ORORO
BEFORE THE STORM

WRITER: Marc Sumerak

PENCILS: Carlo Barberi & Scott Hepburn@UDON

INKS: Robert Campanella, Derek Fridolfs, M3TH@UDON, Andrew Pepoy, John Stanisci & Juan Vlasco

COLORS: Val Staples & Shane Law@UDON

LETTERER: Dave Sharpe

COVERS: Mark Brooks with David McCaig, Randy Green with Rick Ketcham & J. Rauch, Patrick Zircher with Derek Fridolfs & Rob Schwager and Stuart Immonen

EDITOR: Nicole Wiley

CONSULTING EDITORS: MacKenzie Cadenhead & Mark Paniccia

ORORO

BEFORE THE STORM

COLLECTION EDITOR: Jennifer Grünwald
ASSISTANT EDITOR: Michael Short
SENIOR EDITOR, SPECIAL PROJECTS: Jeff Youngquist
DIRECTOR OF SALES: David Gabriel
PRODUCTION: Loretta Krol

BOOK DESIGNER: Carrie Beadle
CREATIVE DIRECTOR: Tom Marvelli

EDITOR IN CHIEF: Joe Quesada
PUBLISHER: Dan Buckley

#1

Mexico
The Temple of Huitzilopochtli

Almost there...
...almost--
RMMBLLLLL
Oh, man... not another one...
CLICK!
Okay, I get it--
--unh!--
--the Aztec God of War isn't fond of intruders!
Hmmm...
That wasn't nearly as bad as the legends made it out to be...

Now all that's left between me and certain glory--
--is one last leap of--
SNAP
--NO!
NNnnnhh...
If anyone's listening...
...I could use a hand here!
I can see that, doctor.
I take it from the destruction in your wake that you were able to locate the artifact?
...NNnHH...

It was...Nnnn... right where the manuscripts said it would be, Barrett.
I'll give it to you...Nnhhh!... as soon as you help me up!
The artifact first, doctor.
Heh... you're insane, Barrett!
And you are in no position to argue, I'm afraid...
Finally...
...La Corona de Huitzilopochtli...
With this, the world is one step away from apocalypse...
Barrett-- please!
...a shame you won't live to see it, doctor...
AAAAHHHHH!

Egypt
Cairo's Market District
I am going back in.

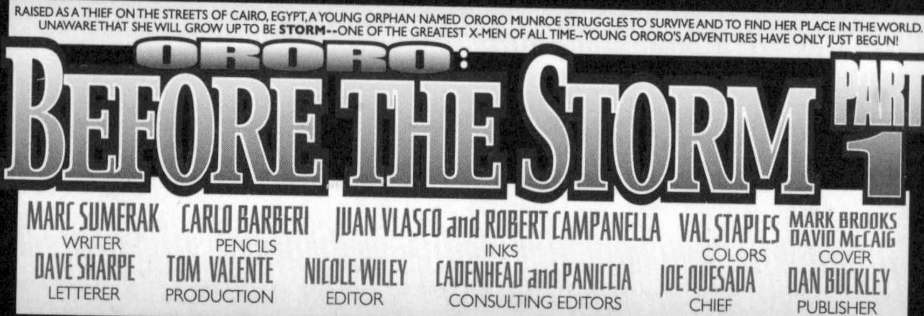
RAISED AS A THIEF ON THE STREETS OF CAIRO, EGYPT, A YOUNG ORPHAN NAMED ORORO MUNROE STRUGGLES TO SURVIVE AND TO FIND HER PLACE IN THE WORLD. UNAWARE THAT SHE WILL GROW UP TO BE STORM--ONE OF THE GREATEST X-MEN OF ALL TIME--YOUNG ORORO'S ADVENTURES HAVE ONLY JUST BEGUN!
ORORO:
BEFORE THE STORM PART 1
MARC SUMERAK WRITER
CARLO BARBERI PENCILS
JUAN VLASCO and ROBERT CAMPANELLA INKS
VAL STAPLES COLORS
MARK BROOKS DAVID McCAIG COVER
DAVE SHARPE LETTERER
TOM VALENTE PRODUCTION
NICOLE WILEY EDITOR
CADENHEAD and PANICCIA CONSULTING EDITORS
JOE QUESADA CHIEF
DAN BUCKLEY PUBLISHER

Do not be foolish, Ororo.
Imagine what Teacher will do if we are caught!
His punishment will be much worse if we return without enough food for everyone, Nari.
Now, stay silent...
...this will not take long...

Nari--
what are you
doing?
We are
going home,
Hakiim.
But what
about--
Leave the
"master thief"
to fend for
herself.
Why must
you be so
jealous?
Teacher picked
Ororo to lead us
because she--
Still your
tongue!
SWAK!
No!
What have
you--
THUD!
Eh?
What
was--
Goddess!

Quickly!
Thief!
My apologies, Ororo! It seems Hakiim's carelessness has once again--
Nari!
Enough! We have no time to waste in argument!
Stick to the rooftops...
...and pray to the Bright Lady that our feet are swifter than theirs!
There they are!
Follow them!
Jump, Hakiim!

I...I...
You know he will not make it, Ororo.
We should just leave him behind before we all get--
Do not listen to her, Hakiim.
I believe you can do it! I believe in you!
Now jump!
THUDD!
UNNNGH!
So much for believing...
Hakiim, are you--?
I...am fine...
...I think...
Now come, Ororo! We have a job to finish!
I will not suffer for Hakiim's mistakes!
That is where we are different, Nari.

I would suffer far more if I knew I had left a friend behind!
SWOOSH!
I am here, Hakiim.
...thank you...
Halt, thieves!
Do not thank me quite yet...

Well, well...
...what have we here?
Prepare to find out!
Ororo!
Ha! I could have sworn we were looking for real thieves!
Turns out we've only got ourselves a little rat problem.
Do you know what we do when we find rats with our food, little ones?
No...
...but I am sure it is nothing that you would regret later...

Achmed El-Gibar!
W-we are done for!
Forgive me, sir! I was merely doing my duty!
I did not realize these children were under your protection!
An honest mistake, my friend.
One that can easily be remedied...
Anything you wish, sir. All that is mine is yours!
You have acted wisely this night, gentlemen. The same cannot be said for my pupils.
Deal with them as you wish...
...if you can find them...

Soon...
The guards had surrounded us--
--fifteen or twenty of them--
--and I knew we were in trouble!
Then what happened, Nari?
Luckily, I managed to clear a path through them... but Ororo wanted to stay and fight!
I knew it was more important to deliver this food to all of you, so I escaped while I still could!
Are you sure, Nari? Ororo would never put herself before--
Ha! You must be as foolish as Hakiim!
Being Achmed's prize pupil has gone straight to Ororo's head.
All she is after is glory!
Funny...
...I was just thinking the same thing about you.

Ororo! Hakiim!
I was just telling the others about... how glorious... you were this evening...
Nari! How-- how dare you?!
You--you abandon us to save yourself, and then spread lies to save face!
What?
Would you rather that I told them that your lack of skill is the reason their bellies will be less full tonight?
That's it!
Calm, Hakiim.
This is not a fight worth having. Not now.
You may be able to run from me...
...but Teacher will have your head for your failure tonight!
Who will be praised and who will be punished is not for you to decide, little urchin.

Teacher!
Welcome home, Master El-Gibar!
I stole this just for you!
Eat, my children.
I see that all of you have earned your keep this day...
...well, almost all of you...
But, Master!
I was the only one to escape with the spoils!
I have taught you to steal for survival, Nari...
...but I never taught you to steal away when your fellow thieves need you!
As for you, Hakiim...it seems that once again you have failed to--
No, Teacher. Hakiim was merely following my orders.
This was all my fault. I am sorry.
I must admit, I expect better from you, Ororo.
Perhaps an evening without supper will help you to learn from your mistakes...

Later...
My mother always said that the Goddess smiled upon this land.
On a night like this, I can almost understand what she meant.
It almost makes you forget our place in the world for a moment...
...don't you agree, Hakiim?
I was that obvious, eh?
Maybe Nari was right-- I really do make a lousy thief!
Perhaps I should stop pushing my luck and look for another way of life before it is too late!

You do not have to be so hard on yourself...
And you did not have to take the blame for my blunders.
Not that I didn't appreciate it...
Here...I brought you this.
No, Hakiim. My punishment is--
At least half of your punishment should be mine!
So in return, at least half of my supper should be yours!
You...you are a good friend, Hakiim.
And in this life, that is the greatest treasure.
Then come back inside where many more friends await you!
No matter how hard you gaze, there is nothing out there but sand and stars...
I am beginning to think you are right...
Then why have so many of your nights been spent up here alone staring off into the nothingness?

My mother used to tell me that I was destined for great things.
She said that the blood of queens and priestesses flowed in my veins...
...if she could only see me now.
Every night I hear her words echoing in my head like a distant song, and I wait for the nothingness to finally give way to something more.
It never does.
You really miss them, don't you?
Yes. I do.
Even though I was there when they--
--I...I still dream my parents will return some day. That they are still out there somewhere... alive...
Consider yourself lucky. My parents--they abandoned me when I was just a baby.
As much as I wish that I could understand your pain...
...I have never even had anyone to miss...
Then you may truly be the luckiest of us all...

The Marketplace, The Next Morning...
Simply *amazing*...
Fine antiques!
Fresh fruit! Fresh dates!
...and to *think*, the *guidebook* said the *market* was *dangerous* for *tourists!*

Not bad for one morning...
Oh-- excuse me, sir!
Not so fast, little one...
...I believe that you and I have some unfinished business to take care of!
You!
You can't escape me this time, child!

Another dead end!
Perfect...
I've got you now, you little--
Huh? Where did she--
--Ah!
Seems our little rat still likes the high life!
Well, this time there is no escape!

Now, urchin, prepare to meet your--
Gone?
But how?!?
No...
Curse you, child!!!

Whew...
That was far too close...
...if I had to hide in that pot any longer I might have--
--afraid you will have to look elsewhere, my friend.
Teacher?
Mr. El-Gibar, I've been told that your thieves are the best Cairo has to offer.
I am sorry. What you have described is far too dangerous!
I thought you might feel that way...
...but I can assure you, your services would be repaid beyond your wildest dreams!
I see.
In that case, Mr. Barrett...
...I think I may have just the thief you are looking for!

#2

Not much further...
ORORO:
BEFORE THE STORM PART 2
MARC SUMERAK
WRITER
CARLO BARBERI
PENCILS
JUAN VLASCO
INKS
VAL STAPLES
COLORS
RANDY GREEN, RICK KETCHAM and SOTOCOLOR'S J. RAUCH
COVER
DAVE SHARPE
LETTERER
JARED OSBORN
PRODUCTION
NICOLE WILEY
EDITOR
CADENHEAD and PANICCIA
CONSULTING EDITORS
JOE QUESADA
CHIEF
DAN BUCKLEY
PUBLISHER

NO!
This ends now, Ororo!
There is no escape, my friend.
You have something that belongs to Master El-Gibar...and unless you return it to us now, we will be forced to take it from you!
You know that I have only done what I must, Hakiim...
I expect no less from you.
Then...I am sorry, Ororo...
ENOUGH!
The time for words is long gone. Teacher will not accept failure!
Neither will I...

GET HER!
UNFFH!
I wish it did not have to be this way...
As do I, Hakiim.
But the choice is not ours to make.
OOOF!

And so it is just you and I, Nari.
I would not have it any other way, "sister"...
HYAH!
So... this is all that Teacher's "prize pupil" has to offer?
That title should belong to someone who has earned it!
Yes...
...it should.
Anyone else want to try for it?

There will be no more fighting tonight, my children.
Teacher!
Master El-Gibar!
Now, Ororo...
I believe you have something that belongs to me?
Yes, Teacher...
...here it is, safe and sound.
Wonderful!
It seems you have beaten your own record, little one!
I am going to have to make this test more difficult next time...
I pray that you will be able to work with your fellow urchins as well as you work against them...

"...for tomorrow, a completely different kind of test is about to begin!"
Dr. Barrett-- your guests have arrived!
Ah! Master El-Gibar! So good to see you again!
I assume you've brought the...special help that I requested?

Of course.
The greatest thieves in all of Cairo, at your service...
Children--?
Achmed, my good man, may I have a word with you?
In private?!
Did we do something wrong?
No, Hakiim. I do not believe it is our actions that we are being judged on...
My apologies, friends.
When I was told that your Master was the portal to Egypt's finest thieves, I naturally assumed that his students would be a bit...older.
An honest mistake...one you can surely understand.
But Mr. El-Gibar assures me that you are indeed the best that Cairo has to offer...
...and that is exactly what this mission shall require!
And what is it that we are to do?

Within the ruins of this ancient temple lies a stone once thought to possess great powers--
--the Opal of Ozymandias.
Legend says that he who possesses the Opal will become invincible. Immortal.
That he will live eternally in the service of an ancient Egyptian warlord called En Sabah Nur!
So...is that why you want this stone?
You want to become the invincible servant of...whatever his name was?
Ha! Of course not, child! That is just the stuff of myths!
I merely seek to safely deliver this priceless artifact into a museum before it falls into the hands of some filthy local scoundrel too savage to understand its true glory!
Umm...and by that, I wasn't referring to any of you, of course...

Why not just retrieve the Opal yourself?
I'm...a bit past my adventuring days, I'm sad to say.
The temple is riddled with booby traps and dangers that only the most skilled thieves could possibly hope to survive...
...and then there's the curse...
Did you say... curse?!
No need to worry, little one!
Most of these old Egyptian "curses" are nothing more than exaggerated "no trespassing" signs.
And what does this one say?
Let's see...
"Ozymandias the Eternal will give life to the stones themselves so to crush all who invade the sanctum of En Sabah Nur."
Or something close to that...my hieroglyphics are a bit rusty...
I assure you, though... in all my years in the field, I've never found a "curse" actually worth worrying about!
Booby traps, on the other hand, are a different story...

And if we manage to find this bauble you seek--
--if we willingly risk our lives only to further your pursuit of glory--
--what exactly do we receive in return?
Ororo!
Easy, Achmed.
Your pupil asks a wise question!
You need not fear, young one.
Not only will you be forever remembered for helping bring the wonders of a long-lost culture to today's world--
--but you and your brethren shall also be rewarded in ways far more grand than you ever imagined possible!
Well, Ororo... now what do you have to say?
When do we begin?

Soon...
The map says we should head for a corridor down this way...
Hakiim, stay close to us!
We don't know what might await us in--
GAAAHHH!
HAKIIM!
Relax, Hakiim! It is only a statue!
No matter how ugly it is, it cannot hurt you!
If you react like this now, how can you possibly face the real danger ahead?
I will be fine, Nari. Worry about yourself.
I wonder why Teacher even made us bring you! It is bad enough that I have to work side-by-side with--
--Ororo?
Hmm. Where did she--?

Oh no... not you too!
I...I am sorry.
I do not do well with... such small places.
What is the matter, Ororo? Afraid the ceiling is going to come crashing down on you?
NARI!
How pathetic! If I were you, I would instead fear Teacher's reaction when he finds out that you--
SLAM!
I have my reasons.
Now, kindly give me a moment and we will move on.
It is okay, Ororo.
I will be right here with you.
Thank you, Hakiim.

I do not understand what the problem is...
...there is nothing at all to be afraid of down--
--here?
SNAP!!
No!
NAR!!
The ceiling!

RUN!
THOOM
JUMP!
THOOM
THOOM

I... I...
You are safe...
...for now...
The curse!
It said that the stones would come to life and crush all invaders!
So...that was it?
How disappointing.
Scorpions?!
Do not fret, Hakiim.
It seems that we have plenty more ahead of us to keep us on our toes.

Th-they look hungry!
And I hear they love the taste of scared little boys!
Wha--?!
Don't listen to her, Hakiim. Just get across the bridge.
And don't look--
SNAP!
Hakiim!
YAAAHHH!
H-help me!
Give me your hand!
HSSSS!
Nnnh... got you...
At least we can be sure of one thing...
It cannot get any worse than this!

Come, Achmed. It is getting late.
My men will return you to Cairo before nightfall.
No...I think I shall remain until my students emerge.
But it could be hours more. Surely you have more important things to--
I said I will remain.
I understand. You are worried about them.
As any father worries for his children.
But they are well prepared. I know they will succeed.
As do I...
...as do I...

"It cannot get any worse than this!"
You just had to open your big mouth, eh, Hakiim?
And if you do not close yours, Nari, I will be glad to do it for you!
Ha! I would like to see you try, you little--
Quiet, you two...
...we're almost there!

At last!
The main chamber! The map says this is where the Opal should be!
Then let's get this over with already!
Nari! Be careful!
There are bound to be more traps surrounding the Opal!
You be as careful as you want, Ororo.
I have a job to do.

But Nari--!
Let her go.
And now to claim the prize!
Eww. This statue guy is so creepy.
But the Opal--
--it's beautiful!
See, Ororo? I told you!
Nothing happened at all!

Now, let's get out of this place and claim our reward!
Oh, what is the matter now?
Nari--the statues!
I already told you, Hakiim...
...they're nothing but stone...

...there's *no way* they can *hurt* us!

#3

My students have been gone for far too long...
Something must be wrong!
Dr. Barrett, I--
--and as soon as those whelps return with the Opal, we begin the ceremony!
Soon, our Dark Master shall rise again...
...and we shall serve at his side as he ushers in a new Age of Apocalypse!
NO!
Eh?

I should never have trusted him!
I must find the children!
WARN THEM!
THWAK!
I'm sorry, my friend...
...but I can't allow you to do that.
After all, we still need you alive...
...nNNnnHhh...
...well, at least for now...

ORORO:
BEFORE THE STORM

We're dead!

Try not to lose hope, Hakiim!
As long as we stand, we may still stand a chance!

PART 3
MARC SUMERAK
WRITER
CARLO BARBERI and SCOTT HEPBURN
PENCILS
JUAN VLASCO and UDON
INKS
SHANE LAW@UDON
COLORS
ZIRCHER, FRIDOLFS and SCHWAGER COVER
DAVE SHARPE
LETTERER
JAMES TAVERAS
PRODUCTION
NICOLE WILEY
EDITOR
CADENHEAD and PANICCIA
CONSULTING EDITORS
JOE QUESADA
CHIEF
DAN BUCKLEY
PUBLISHER
Who are you trying to kid, Ororo?
For once, Hakiim may be right!
THOOOOM!

These stone creatures may be bigger and stronger than us--
--but we are smarter and faster!
THWAMM!
Some of us are smart enough to know we cannot beat these things!
And perhaps we would not have to if you had been more careful, Nari!

The curse spoke of "living stones," Hakiim! These must be the Opal's guardians!
And that one over there seems to be in charge!
Well, the Opal is ours now...and none of them can take it--
--uh-oh.
THOOM
CRSSHH
RMMBLLL
Ha!
It looks like once again I have--
--spoken too soon...

HAKIM!
I could use some help here!
THWAM THWAM THWAM THWAM
That's right...over here, ugly...
KRAKT!
You are not the only one!
Come on!
Hit me with your best shot!

HAKIIM--
KRAKK!
--JUMP!
Thank you, Nari.
I owe you one.
Yeah, yeah...
Just don't tell anyone, okay?

This is it, Ororo...
...one last chance.
It's either you--
SMASH!
--or her!
Three down...
...way down...
...and one to--
Ororo!
--no!

Let us go!
This has gone too far.
The Opal?!
Ororo! What are you doing?
Saving your life...
...I hope...
Release them at once, or your prize will follow its guardian into the depths below!
Well played, child...

...but the time for games is over.
Release me!
Now, bring her here, my stone horseman.
Let Ozymandias have a better look at this foolish little--
gasp!
Wait! It cannot be!
So young... but there is no mistake!
Ozymandias begs your forgiveness, my child.
He mistook you for a common intruder.
He did not expect you...not so soon...
Huh?!

You are Ozymandias?
Then, this temple--the Opal--they belong to you?
Nothing belongs to Ozymandias, child. Not even his own life.
His Master--En Sabah Nur--made sure of that centuries ago.
Now, Ozymandias is no different from the statues at his command. He is naught but a humble servant.
Today, he serves you.
But why? Why do you bow to me?
Who do you think I am?
Ozymandias knows not only who you are, child--
--but also who you will become!

The stones do not lie!
That is... me?
But... how?!?
Ozymandias sees all.
Visions of the future that he carves on the stone helix.
A record of what has passed and what will be, etched in eternity, waiting for En Sabah Nur to rise again.
It is the gift-- and the curse-- his master has bestowed upon him.

Those visions have shown Ozymandias that your path will be a long and difficult one.
That the trials you have already faced in life are nothing compared to the ones ahead of you.
But they also show that you will prevail.
That you will soar on the winds as a savior of your people.
You must be mistaken.
I am an orphan. I have no people...
Not yet, perhaps.
But you will find them someday... and you will help lead them to a brighter tomorrow.
You, child, are destined for great things.
You are one of the chosen.
I...I am?

Your journey has just begun...
...and today, fate has brought you here for a reason.
The Opal?
It is yours to take. Ozymandias now sees why you must...
...but be warned--its power comes with a terrible price!
Now, go! Destiny awaits you beyond these walls...
Hey!
Oof!
You heard him! Come, Ororo!
But Ozymandias--how may we return your kindness?
Worry not...
...I am certain that your debt to En Sabah Nur will be repaid in full...
...someday...

Elsewhere...
Still awake, Abdul?
Yes. Teacher and the others--
--they have not yet returned.
They are probably off on another grand adventure.
You need not worry! They can take care of themselves!
I suppose you are right...
Of course I am!
Now, come away from that window already...
...unless there is something exciting happening outside I don't know about!
No...
...there never is...

The Temple
So...
...is anyone else having a hard time believing what just happened back there?
I am not sure any of us truly understands what is going on, Hakiim.
No?
Well, maybe we could figure it out if you would tell us every-thing that stone freak said to you, Ororo!
He... he told me what I needed to hear.
Nothing more.
Just let it go, Nari!
We have the Opal...that's all that matters right now.
The sooner we get out of here, the--

KZZZAT!
--eh?
Uh-oh!
Another trap?!
KRASHH!
Look out!

Ororo?
koff
Hakiim?
koff
koff
Are you--
No!
Teacher!
Come quick!
Help!
Ah! You have returned safely!
How... delightful...

Please, sir! You must hurry!
Something has gone terribly wrong!
You were able to find the Opal?
Yes, but--
Then we have nothing to worry about.
You do not understand! Ororo and Hakiim have been hurt!
We triggered another booby trap and--
I'm afraid that you are mistaken.
No, I am not!
I saw it with my own eyes! They were--
Buried alive beneath a ton of rubble?
I know. That's exactly what I intended.
W-what?!

You and your friends have already seen far too much.
I couldn't risk you disrupting my plans.
And while your skills may have been necessary to retrieve the Opal--
--in the end, you are all quite expendable.
I never expected any of you would be quick enough to escape...
...but I must say, I do appreciate you saving my men the trouble of digging this out!
You...
...you set this trap?
Foolish child...

Achmed!
I am the trap.
Your Master can't hear you, little one.
But don't worry...
...you'll be with him very soon...
KZZZAT!

#4

It seems like a lifetime ago.
Everything was perfect...
...until the sky fell.
When the dust finally cleared, my life was forever changed...
M-Mother...?
...and the people I loved had paid the price.
MOTHER!
It was my darkest day...

...and now, history is repeating itself!
HAKIIM?!
...nnnNNnn...
Hold on, Hakiim!
I am coming for you! I--
--no! Too heavy!
Can't... pull free...
Goddess-- please! Help us!
This... this cannot be happening...
...not again...
...never again...

ORORO:
BEFORE THE STORM
PART 4
MARC SUMERAK WRITER
CARLO BARBERI PENCILS
ANDREW PEPOY, JOHN STANISCI and M3TH INKS
SHANE LAW@UDON COLORS
STUART IMMONEN COVER
DAVE SHARPE LETTERER
TOM VALENTE PRODUCTION
NICOLE WILEY EDITOR
CADENHEAD and PANICCIA CONSULTING EDITORS
JOE QUESADA CHIEF
DAN BUCKLEY PUBLISHER
What...
...what just happened?
Where is--

--HAKIIM!
Are you all right?
Please, Hakiim--answer me!
I am...a bit sore...but I'll survive.
I will take a few bruises over being buried alive any day!
Um...speaking of which...how did we get free?
It sounded like a storm erupted inside the temple!
I wish I had an answer.
I called to the Goddess, begging for her mercy, and then--
It seems that she was listening.
That is answer enough for me.

TEACHER! NARI!
No need to worry any longer! We are--
Wait! Where has everyone gone?
It is late. Perhaps they are just off getting some rest?
Teacher would never rest if he knew we were in danger.
Something is very wrong here...
...and we are going to find out what it is.
Barrett's tent? Are you sure we should go in there, Ororo?
Where better to start than with the man who brought us here in the first place?
I have a bad feeling about this.
As do I, Hakiim...
As do--

--oof!
Who?!
AAAIIEEEE!
Unnh!
THWAM!
You will pay for what you have done this night, you vile--
Abdul?!?
HAKIIM! ORORO!
I...I am sorry! I thought that they had returned for me!
If I had known it was you, I never would have--
But they said you were dead...and I was afraid that if they found me--
Hold on...who said we were dead?
And how did you get here? Where is Master El-Gibar?
Tell us, Abdul--what is going on?

A group of men broke into our den while we were sleeping.
They took us by surprise. Tied us up and brought us here.
I managed to slip free and hide as the others were being unloaded.
Master El-Gibar and Nari were already being held prisoner when we arrived.
And the man in white, he...he said that he had killed you both!
Barrett? Then it must have been him that trapped us in the temple!
And the others? Where are they now, Abdul?
The guards took them into this other tent over here, but they...they never came out.
I was...too afraid to follow them in alone.
There is no need to be afraid any-more.
We go in together...
...and we do not return until every last one of us is safe!

Soon...
After all these years of research and sacrifice, the pieces are finally in place!
Once this ancient equipment is assembled, the resurrection can begin.
With the life force of these pathetic urchins to provide him sustenance, En Sabah Nur--the first of my kind--will soon rise again...
...and the glory of the Apocalypse will be unleashed!
And now, thanks to the combined powers of the Opal and the Crown, I will be able to serve my Dark Lord for all eternity!
Invincible.
Immortal.
Unstoppable!

This is the "great reward" Barrett promised us? To become human sacrifices for some super-mummy?
The man is obviously beyond reason...
...which is why we need to stop him now--before it is too late!
I will provide a distraction while the two of you try to free the--
No, Ororo. Let me distract the guards.
I may not have been brave enough to save my brothers before, but now is my chance to make amends.
This is not the time for--
Yes. It is.
And besides, Barrett still believes that you are dead!
Until you reveal yourself, the element of surprise is still in our hands.
You are right, Abdul.
May the others see your courage as clearly as I do.

The equipment is nearly assembled, Dr. Barrett.
Good. And the children?
They are a fiery lot...but we have them under control.
Perhaps you have spoken too soon, dog!
How--?
He--he must have slipped away earlier!
It doesn't matter, you idiot! Just get him!
I can't allow my plans to be ruined by a mere child!
Not when I am so close to eternal glory!

I have to give the child credit. He's got guts!
Too bad they'll soon be spilled all over the cavern floor!
My students are far more capable than you imagine...
...as you will soon discover...
UGH!
KRAKT!
THWAK!
Ennh!
These old eyes are warmed by the sight of you, my children.
Now, we must move quickly and quietly...

"...Abdul will not last forever on his own..."
This is the best you can do?
GAHH!
Oof!
Come on, guys! There are four of you...
...and I'm only ten years--
KZZAATTT!
Enough!
This nuisance will end now...
...even if I have to kill the child myself.
You can try, Barrett...

...but this time, I suggest that you finish the job.

As you wish.
KZAATT!
KZAATT!
You have made us all proud today, Abdul.
Thank you, Teacher!
KRAK!
I thought I might never see you again, Ororo...
KZAATT!
Ha! If only you were so lucky, Nari!
KZAATT!

These brats are ruining every-thing!
But even if I cannot return En Sabah Nur to power today, the power of the Opal is still within my--
--grasp?
No! The Opal! It's--
Looking for this?
KZAATT!
KZAATT!
I'll take that as a "yes"...

Get down from there!
What is the matter, Barrett?
Afraid you might accidentally hit your "Dark Lord"?
Eww...
Why you would want to spend all eternity looking at this face is beyond me!
You may have found safe haven for the moment, child...
...but your friends have not!
NARI!

It seems the tables have turned, little one.
Give me the Opal at once-- or the girl dies.
And then the rest of your worthless "family" follows...
...one at a time...
...nnh hhh...
But, if I give you the Opal--
--what will stop you from killing us anyway?
I...I don't know what to do...
You have done your part, Hakiim.
Now let me do mine.
My pleasure...

If what you said is true, Barrett, this stone will grant you immortality.
That should give you plenty of time to try to bring your master back to life again.
So, I offer you a trade-- the Opal for our insignificant lives.
It is the least you can do after our service to you--and to En Sabah Nur-- this day.
Yes...I suppose that is fair.
After all, no power comes without a price...
So I've been warned.

And now, children--witness my ascent to eternal glory!
Behold me as the world shall know me from this day forward!
Today, I finally shed my mortal skin and am remade in the true image of--
Wait! What--
What is happening to me?!
I...I can't move!
The legends--they promised I would live forever!
This can't be--

He--he turned to stone?!
I guess he got his immortality... just not in the way he expected!
So much for not believing in curses...
How did you know that was going to happen, Ororo?
I...I didn't...
WHAT?
When Ozymandias gave me the Opal, he warned me that its powers came at a great cost.
I had no choice but to hope that he was not exaggerating.
Luckily, he was not.
It was quite a risk...but one worth taking, it seems.
Now, let us leave this place. You can tell us more about your adventures...
"...once we are all safely back home..."

The next day...
You are unusually quiet, Hakiim. Is everything all right?
A man tried to kill us and then turned to stone in front of our eyes.
You tell me, Ororo...
Perhaps there are some things we are not meant to understand.
But I have faith that all the answers will be revealed to us over time.
Well, I do know one thing--you saved us all! More than once!
You said that your mother used to tell you that you were destined for great things?
I think that today you have proven her words true.
He is right for once, you know...
Nari!
...just don't tell the others that I said so, okay?
You have my word... "sister"...

So...
With Barrett, um, out of the picture, what do you think will happen to the Opal now?
"I do not know, Hakiim...
"...but I have a feeling it will someday find its way back to where it belongs.
"Hopefully, we will as well."
The Beginning...